simple machines

Ramps and Wedges

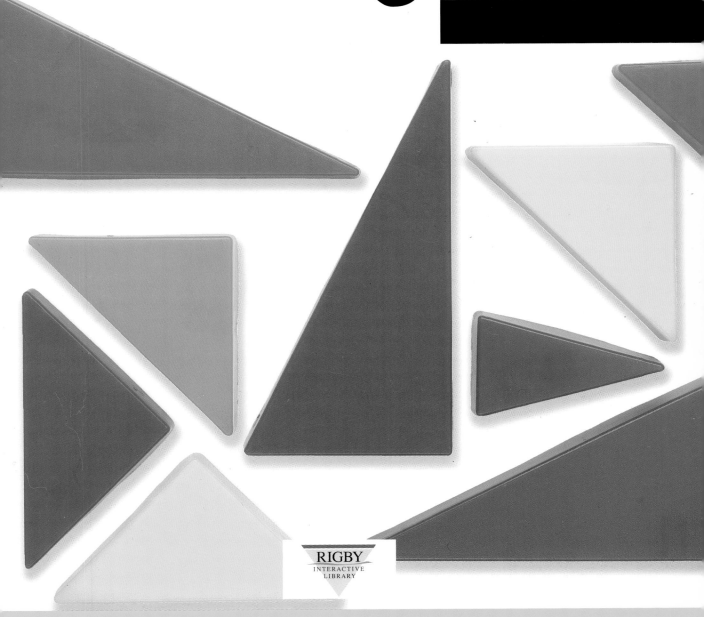

RIGBY
INTERACTIVE
LIBRARY

David Glover

This edition © 1997 Rigby Education
Published by Rigby Interactive Library,
an imprint of Rigby Education,
division of Reed Elsevier, Inc.
Chicago, IL

Customer Service 888-454-2279

Visit our website at www.heinemannlibrary.com

Designed by Celia Floyd and Sharon Rudd
Illustrated by Barry Atkinson (pp. 13, 14, 21) and Tony Kenyon (pp. 5, 6, 11)
Printed in Hong Kong/China

06 05 04 03 02
10 9 8 7 6 5 4

Library of Congress Cataloging-in-Publication Data
Glover, David.
     Ramps and Wedges/David Glover.
          p.   cm. — (Simple machines)
     Includes index.
     Summary: Uses a variety of examples, from scissors and axes to zippers and hairpin turns,

to demonstrate the power of the inclined plane and show how ramps and wedges make work

and play easier.
     ISBN 1–57572–083–3 (lib. bdg.)   ISBN 1–4034–0058–X (pbk. bdg.)
     1. Simple machines—Juvenile literature. 2. Inclined planes—Juvenile literature.

3. Wedges—Juvenile literature. [1. Inclined planes. 2. Wedges.] I. Title. II. Series.
     TJ147.G58   1997
     621.8 ' 11—dc20

96-17486
CIP
AC

Acknowledgments
The Publishers would like to thank the following for permission to reproduce photographs:
Trevor Clifford, pp. 4, 5, 14, 15, 16, 20; Zefa, pp. 7, 8, 12; Jess Stock/TSW, p. 9; Sue Cunningham, p. 11; J Ringland/TRIP, p. 13; Leonard Lee Rue/Bruce Coleman Ltd., p. 17; Colorsport, pp. 10, 18, 19; Mary Evans Picture Library, p. 22; Robin Smith/TSW, p. 23.

Cover photograph by Trevor Clifford

Some words are shown in bold, **like this.** You can find out what they mean by looking in the glossary.

Contents

What Are Ramps and Wedges?

A ramp is a slope that can be used for moving heavy things up and down. It is much easier to push something up a gentle ramp than up a steep one.

Less effort

When you push an object along a ramp, it goes up gradually. You use less **effort** than when you lift the load straight up into the air.

A wedge is a small ramp that can be moved. It is easy to slide a wedge under a door. The wedge **jams** the door open.

Old and New Ramps

How did the ancient Egyptians lift
huge stones to build the **pyramids?**
They built ramps. Teams of workers
dragged the stones up the ramps.
They took the ramps away when a
pyramid was finished.

Many buildings have ramps for people in wheelchairs. Gentle ramps allow them to go up and down without having to use stairs.

FACT FILE

Pyramid power

The Great Pyramids of Egypt are nearly 5,000 years old. Every stone was moved by people or animals. Then there were no bulldozers, trucks, or cranes.

Up and Down Hills

It is hard work to climb a steep hill. Your body has to lift a long way with each step. A **zig-zag** path up a hill takes you steadily to the top. You have to walk a longer distance than if you go straight up, but each step is easier.

Skiers move in zig-zags to come down a steep slope. If they skied straight down, they would go too fast and might crash. The zig-zags help them to come down safely.

FACT FILE

Hairpin turns

Roads zig-zag up steep hills so that cars can climb them more easily. The sharp bends between the zig-zags are called *hairpin turns.*

Blocks and Chocks

Athletes use wedge-shaped blocks at the start of a race. They are called *starting blocks*. Runners push off against them to get a quick start.

This man is using metal wedges to split a block of stone. When he hammers the wedges into the stone, the wedge splits the stone apart.

FACT FILE

Chocks away!

Chocks are wedges placed under the wheels of airplanes. They stop the plane from moving until the pilot is ready. Years ago, when the pilot wanted to take off, he shouted 'Chocks away!'

Axes and Plows

An axe is a sharp metal wedge that is fixed to a handle. The handle lets a farmer swing the axe head to hit a log with great force. The sharp wedge-shaped blade of the axe cuts into the wood and splits it apart.

The first axes

Simple stone axes were made by the first human beings hundreds of thousands of years ago. They tied wedge-shaped pieces of stone to wooden handles.

Farmers use **plows** to turn the soil. A plow has blades that cut into the soil. These blades are metal wedges. They make lines called **furrows.** This tractor is pulling a plow with several blades.

Knives and Scissors

When your mom or dad cuts a carrot with a knife, the blade works as a wedge. The sharp edge of the blade is very thin. It cuts easily into the carrot. The knife blade gets thicker away from the sharp edge. It forces the carrot apart.

Scissors are a pair of blades with sharp wedge-shaped edges. The blades work together to cut paper or cloth.

Shears are powerful scissors with curved blades. They are used to cut twigs and branches.

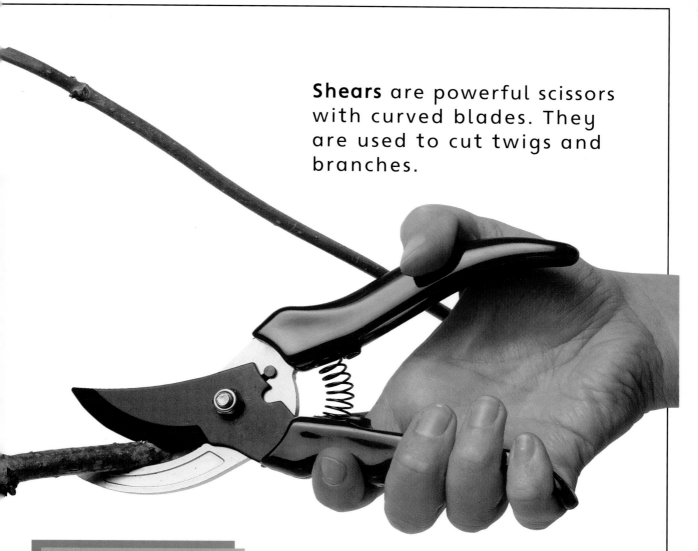

FACT FILE

Hedge trimmers

A hedge trimmer has lots of wedge-shaped blades. A **motor** moves the blades backward and forward at high speeds.

Teeth

Feel the shape of your front teeth.
They are wedges with sharp edges.
You use these teeth to cut and bite
your food. You can
feel how they
work when
you take a
bite from
an apple.

Rats and mice have sharp teeth for nibbling and gnawing their food. Beavers can cut through tree trunks with their powerful wedge-shaped teeth. They use the wood they cut to build their river homes.

Giant Jumps

This water skier is jumping off a ramp. The skier comes up to the ramp at high speed. The slope of the ramp lifts him into the air.

This acrobatic skier is using a steep snow ramp to jump high into the air. He will be able to make amazing twists and turns before landing.

FACT FILE

Ski jumps

An expert water skier can use a ramp to jump half the length of a football field.

Zippers

It is hard to close a zipper without the **slider.** Two wedges inside the slider press the teeth together when you zip it up. A third wedge pushes the teeth apart when you pull the slider down.

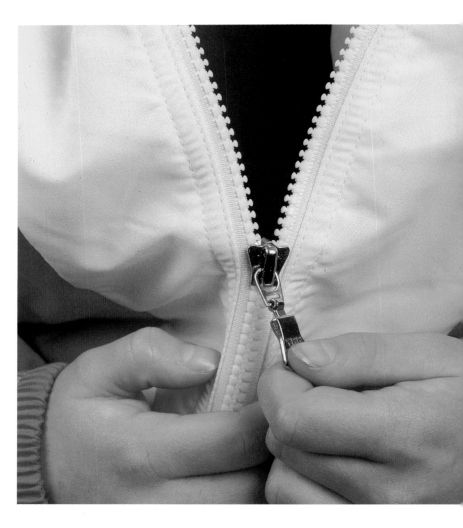

FACT FILE

The first zipper

The zipper was invented in 1891 by Whitcomb Judson, an American. The first zippers were used to fasten boots.

The teeth on a zipper are shaped so that they fit together. A bump on one tooth fits into a dent on the next tooth.

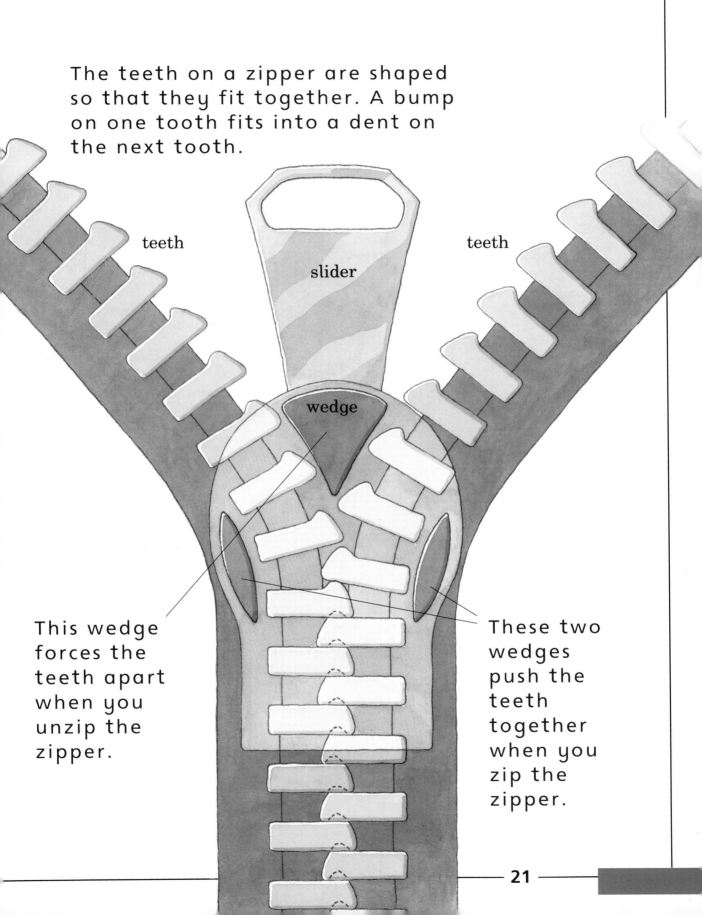

teeth

slider

teeth

wedge

This wedge forces the teeth apart when you unzip the zipper.

These two wedges push the teeth together when you zip the zipper.

Slides and Rides

Some of the most exciting carnival rides are ramps that you slide down at great speed.

Water slides like this were popular 100 years ago. They are still great fun today. A rope pulls the car to the top of the ramp and then lets the car go.

On a roller coaster, your car
is pulled to the top of a steep
ramp by a powerful engine.
Then you rush down the slope
on the other side. It is both
scary and exciting at the same
time!

Glossary

chocks Wedge-shaped blocks for putting under wheels to stop them from turning **11**

effort Pushing, pulling, or turning force you must make to move something **5**

furrows Straight cuts or grooves in the ground that plows make as they turn the soil **13**

jam To block or wedge in one place **5**

motor Part of a machine that makes it go. Some motors are powered by electricity, others by gasoline **15**

plow Machine with large blades pulled by a horse or a tractor. A farmer uses a plow to turn the soil in the fields. **13**

pyramids Pointed mounds of stone. The ancient Egyptians built huge stone pyramids as places to bury their kings. **6**

slider Part of a zipper that you move up and down to open and close it **20**

slope Ramp or hill **9**

zig-zag Line that turns back and forth, like the letter *z* *8*

Index

Further Readings

Lampton, Christopher. *Bathtubs, Slides, Roller Coaster Rails: Simple Machines That Are Really Inclined Planes.* Brookfield, CT: Millbrook Press, 1991.

William, John. *Simple Science Projects with Machines.* Milwaukee: Gareth Stevens, 1992.